How to Be
SPIRITUAL
Without Being
RELIGIOUS

D. PATRICK MILLER

FOREWORD BY IYANLA VANZANT

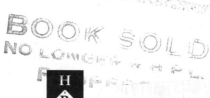

HAMPTON ROADS

Cover design by Laura Beers
Interior by Timm Bryson, em em design LLC
Typeset in 14 point Fournier MT

Hampton Roads Publishing Company, Inc.
Charlottesville, VA 22906
Distributed by Red Wheel/Weiser, LLC
www.redwheelweiser.com

Sign up for our newsletter and special offers by going to *www.redwheel weiser.com/newsletter.*

ISBN: 978-1-57174-842-3
Library of Congress Control Number: 2018954572

Printed in Canada
MAR

10 9 8 7 6 5 4 3 2 1

CONTENTS

Foreword

v

Introduction

ix

I. Releasing Guilt

I

II. Gathering Trust

25

III. Practicing Patience

51

IV. Learning Transcendence

71

V. The Rewards of a Spiritual Faith

105

FOREWORD

In 1999, a small book came across my desk
from a source that is still unknown to me. It
was *The Book of Practical Faith* by D. Patrick
Miller. After glancing through the first three
pages, I closed my office door, armed myself
with multi-colored highlighters and whipped
through the rest of the book in about two
hours. A week later, every member of my
staff had a copy, and an executive order to
read it. Within days, the ten members of the
faculty of the Inner Visions Institute for Spiritual Development had the same response—
perfect! You see, at the time we were
developing the curriculum for a Spiritual

Life Coaching Program that is now eighteen years old. Every student that graduated from the program for the first ten years has read the book. Many of them still quote it at will.

Now retitled *How to Be Spiritual Without Being Religious*, this remains a spirit-filled, God-ordained work. It speaks to so many common issues and some of the most frequently asked questions that arise as one begins or endeavors to deepen their spiritual awareness and connection. Patrick's writing is so clear and heartfelt that it is hard to believe that he did not write the book for you—whoever you are, and wherever you may be on your journey. Having read the original book at least twenty times, I continue to appreciate three qualities of Patrick's writing that are absolutely essential for spiritual teaching. First, his writing is clear. There are no foo-foo terms or mystical lingo. Each word is carefully selected and eloquently placed so that it speaks to your mind and heart simultaneously. Second, the book is perfectly aligned with spiritual law and principle, although he brilliantly never mentions these things by name. To do so, in my assessment, would probably create confusion, sending the reader off to find more information that they would probably never use. Finally, Patrick writes as if he were speaking to an old friend, over a cup of tea, about things he has lived and experienced. His wisdom oozes through the pages, converting even the most dubious doubter into a believer of what he shares.

I have never laid eyes on Patrick Miller. In fact, over the many years I have taught and recommended this book, I believe I have only spoken to him once. Because I could sense that he put his heart and soul into the book, no further contact was required. My soul knows that he is a powerfully masterful and wise teacher. He is a generous and loving soul. He is my brother. I love him, and I love his work. When Patrick wrote to inquire if I would write a foreword for this new edition, I was honored and humbled. When he shared that the publisher was renaming the book, my heart sank, but only for a moment. *How To Be Spiritual Without Being Religious* is absolutely perfect! This title captures what drew me to the book in the first place: spiritual wisdom offered with clarity, without the doom and gloom that often fills the pages of traditionally religious works. Patrick, you are a genius, and I for one thank you for sharing who you are with the world.

Rev. Dr. Iyanla Vanzant, founder; executive director
Inner Visions Institute for Spiritual Development
host, Iyanla Fix My Life *(OWN TV)*

INTRODUCTION

A spiritual faith is a more practical way to deal with everyday life than cynicism, toughness, or defensiveness. Faith can be sensible and savvy, and practicing it daily increases its usefulness and reliability. Yet a spiritual faith is also tinged with mystery, for it is the connection to our unknown potential and the power of creation itself. Spirituality is the way out of misery, the way in to self-knowledge, and the way toward a more fulfilling and effective life.

Most people might define faith religiously, as a "belief in God." This book is about faith as learning to maintain a constant contact with God. By "God" I mean the universal and marvelously creative energy that moves us all. By recognizing and affirming that energy, we can become increasingly peaceful and wise.

Faith is the willingness to take a chance on what we do not yet believe, for the sake of finding greater happiness, and spreading and sharing peace.

Of course, belief and faith in God can coincide, and strengthen each other. But I believe it is also possible to practice faith—to honor, share, and benefit from a spiritual discipline—without any particular religious belief or affiliation. This is my personal experience, and it is what I mean by "how to be spiritual without being religious."

On the other hand, it is easy to see the damage done in the world by people promoting religious beliefs that are not backed up by the practice of a wise and tolerant faith. Thus, practicing a spiritual faith is not the same as holding fast to a religious belief against all the slings and arrows of reality. In fact, faith is weakened by too much believing. Faith is the willingness to take a chance on what we do not yet believe, for the sake of finding greater happiness, and spreading and sharing peace.

I'm convinced that what most people long for is the constant experience of spirituality and faith in their lives. Obviously, few people identify their longings that way; they are more likely to say they seek intimacy, excitement, comfort, wealth, status, or power. But these objectives are longed for because it seems they would supply what is missing in people's lives. In general terms, what people miss is a sense of stability, security, and fulfillment in everyday living.

The great secret of a spiritual faith is that it can supply the core of what we long for. Faith does not replace longing, but it does refocus longing on inner qualities that can be strengthened through contemplation and practice regardless of one's outer circumstances. By supplying the essence of what we deeply seek, faith also reduces our fear, self-absorption, and competitiveness, thus bringing about a greater harmony between people.

The miracle of a well-practiced faith is that it eventually provides rewards that surpass the mere fulfillment of our desires. That is my conclusion after more than thirty years of investigating spirituality as a personal practice. I have written this book to pass on the good news of my experience: that the essence of whatever we long for in life can be attained through practicing faith, and such a practice can be undertaken by anyone with a little willingness to attempt it. Because faith may still be perceived as a vague religious ideal by many—or something that, like blue eyes, you're either born with or you aren't—I've tried to offer pragmatic steps toward the adoption of faith as a spiritual discipline that can be pursued without any particular religious conviction.

Near the end of the classic adventure film *Indiana Jones and the Last Crusade*, the hero faces the last and most fearful of three challenges he must surmount before he can gain entry to the chamber wherein rests the Holy Grail. Earlier the swashbuckling archaeologist has been told that "the search for the cup of Christ is the search for the divine within all of us"—but as we know from Indy's previous adventures, inward searches are not his style.

Standing before a wide, bottomless chasm, he holds a mystical map that inexplicably portrays a knight walking on air across the chasm. Comprehending that must take a "leap of faith," Indy holds his hand to his chest, blinks, gulps, and then takes a big, cinematic step into the void. His foot lands on solid rock. Now, from a perspective changed only a foot or so from a moment before, Indy can clearly see a path that was totally camouflaged from view before his leap of faith. He crosses over and scatters glistening sand behind him to reveal the way to those who will follow.

This scene is a true and accessible illustration of the nature and practicality of faith. The spiritual life requires frequent crossings from the known to the unknown. Ultimately it can provide knowledge of our wholeness, or "holiness," wherein lie our real security, stability, and fulfillment. Like Indy's map, any guide to the unknown is necessarily mystical and suggestive, rather than logical or definitive. And the purpose of faith is not to uphold a prior belief in something already known, but to advance our perspective on what lies ahead. Sometimes a leap of faith affords us only a few inches of progress, yet the subtlest shifts of view can provide enormous insights and a crucial understanding of the path before us. Finally, one who has crossed over a seeming void can help illuminate the way for others who may follow.

With this book I am trying to scatter a little bright sand on the paths across chasms that I have already traversed, and encourage readers to approach the leaps of faith that are theirs to make on their own. This book recommends surrender as the route to power, and inspired risk-taking as the key to security. I hope that readers will examine the path I am describing with curiosity, skepticism, and a sense of adventure—the same qualities that have stood me in good stead in my own research and experience of spirituality.

What I am attempting to describe might also be called a spirituality of ordinary life. My experience with this spirituality arises from a life-long dedication to the big questions: *"Who am I?," "Why are we here?," "What is the best way to be of use?"* I've never traveled to the East, nor surrendered myself to a guru, nor joined any religious organization to pursue these questions. Instead I've investigated them in the midst of trying to make a living, develop healthier relationships, and deal with all the challenges and limitations of being alive on this earth.

Over the last several decades, I've concentrated with greater clarity on the big questions and made them the focus of my profession as a journalist, author, and publisher. I have had personal contact with a number of extraordinary teachers who have significantly influenced my development. What I have to say about spiritual faith thus represents a unique confluence of many voices and perspectives.

For all the problems of Western society at the present time, I feel that one of its great strengths is the opportunity it provides us to merge our dedication to democracy and free-thinking with the world's great spiritual traditions, most of which have tended to be autocratic in nature. This book, like many others in recent years, is part of a nascent tradition that might be called *spiritual democracy*—a path of many influences, a path both practical and profound that can be pursued by anyone in the midst of ordinary life. I hope that my perspective is accurate and compelling enough to encourage others to investigate this priceless path to happiness and wholeness as well.

Four Steps to
Living Spiritually

The following four steps toward a spiritual and practical faith are both sequential and simultaneous. This kind of paradox is often experienced in the process of building faith.

I. Releasing Guilt is the removal of a common obstacle;

II. Gathering Trust increases strength, something akin to spiritual bodybuilding;

III. Practicing Patience changes one's relationship to time, replacing clock-watching with a calm abiding;

and

IV. Learning Transcendence opens one's vision to more frequent and inspiring glimpses of the infinite.

Releasing Guilt

What stands in the way of faith is not cynicism but guilt. While cynicism is a compensation for living faithlessly, it is paradoxically a kind of faith itself. Instead of relying on hope, possibility, and the best in other people, the cynic relies on disappointment, pessimism, and distrust. By maintaining this attitude he hopes to cut his losses and be amply prepared for the next insult or disaster that life sends his way.

Cynicism seems to have a lot going for it in the modern world. Any cynic worth his salt would say it's always been the best policy. I know that I didn't give up cynicism until it utterly failed me as a means of self-protection. I reached a point in life where I had nothing left to lose but life itself, and even that didn't look like much to hold onto. As I began to understand the psychological roots of my physical collapse, it became clear that my cynical, stressful attitudes toward life had delivered me into this catastrophic condition. But that wasn't the biggest surprise I experienced. The real shocker was comprehending that the source of my cynicism was neither the sorry state of the world nor any betrayal I had experienced at the hands of other people. The source of my cynicism was my own guilt: about what I had done and not done with my life, about my family of origin, about my intimate relationships, about sex, about food, about almost anything you could name.

When all this self-judgment became overwhelming, *then* I decided that the world was in terrible shape and that I had to maintain a wary, jaundiced point of view lest I be victimized by someone. All the while, of course, I was the one doing the most damage to myself. It is the peculiar torture of the cynic to be wearing full battle dress on the outside while the enemy is on the inside, ravaging the soul's territory.

Guilt arises from the reluctance to change.

The enemy is guilt. Guilt arises from the reluctance to change. If we harm someone or violate our own inner sense of right and wrong, we should feel a sense of alarm. In response to that internal alarm, we need to acknowledge our error and either correct or try to make up for it. At the very least, we need to start changing inwardly, changing into someone who would not make that mistake again. It's when we don't act inwardly or outwardly that we begin to accumulate guilt.

While it's true that we may finally act responsibly when guilt becomes unbearable, guilt should not be mistaken for a positive motivation in itself. Something else within ourselves—the soul that is always yearning for greater clarity and purposefulness— will eventually recognize that guilt must be released and real change undertaken.

In the choice between guilt and faith lies the world's fate, for faith can conquer all.

The first step toward a spiritual faith is the most radical, for our belief in the value of guilt is incredibly powerful—bred in the bone, it seems. Questioning a single particle of our guilt can seem like heresy, particularly if we have been raised in a religious tradition that teaches themes of sin and guilt. Many people struggle to preserve their religious faith and their guilt at the same time, and in nearly equal proportions. This is highly impractical. Guilt takes up inner psychic space where faith could otherwise abide. Guilt and faith cannot have a peaceful coexistence. In the choice between guilt and faith lies the world's fate, for faith can conquer all. Guilt will sit on its hands and not do a damn thing.

The key to releasing guilt is unbelievably simple, even if the process may be long and difficult. Ask for guilt to be taken away by a power greater than your own, the original creative intelligence that some of us call God. To ask for this divine favor it is not necessary to believe in God; it is only necessary to be willing to change. (Personally,

I believe that a God powerful enough to have created the universe is a God who feels secure enough to help out disbelievers.) The tiniest kernel of a willingness to change is the first seed of faith—and the beginning of the end of guilt.

ENDING THE INNER WAR

To release guilt is not to fight or deny it. Most people cannot remain guilty for very long without fighting the feeling, and this incites an inner war. But it is only an inner surrender that brings about change. When guilt seems implacable and change impossible, it's time to surrender to the obvious: we cannot release our guilt on our own. We must invite assistance from unseen powers.

———

God is a purpose, not a boss or judge.

———

Such assistance arrives on its own schedule, and through subtle means that may escape your notice at first. Someone may begin to treat you more mercifully than before, for instance, and at first you may not relate this change to your prayer for release from guilt. But it is my experience that divine assistance does eventually arrive, and whenever it is recognized, it may be said that the existence of God is proved because God has delivered a change within ourselves that we did not know how to induce alone. When we have found the way to authentic change, we have found the way to a real God.

COMPASSIONATE SELF-RECOGNITION

Guilt is seldom present without its unhappy partner, helplessness. If you are steeped in guilt, you will judge your present condition as unsatisfactory, yet believe that you are either unworthy or incapable of changing for the better.

The willingness to change begins with self-forgiveness—which is not a way of excusing one's problems, but of recognizing them in a compassionate light. To recognize one's flaws and failures mercifully is to acknowledge that we all come by who we are honestly (even if we have a flaw of dishonesty) because we are always trying to do what's best for ourselves. We may be greatly misled by our self-interest, but it is always there, and within it lies the key to productive change.

Compassionate self-recognition allows us to see how we have been serving self-interest in a narrow, conflicted, or counterproductive way. Recognizing and forgiving our selfishness enables us to enlarge, extend, and refine our self-interest. As our self-interest matures, we increasingly find that it matches the interest of the whole human species—and then the interest of nature, of which our species is a part—and then the divine interest of the cosmos.

Guilt keeps us feeling small and lonesome. Compassionate self-recognition, founded on forgiveness, lets us feel at home anywhere and everywhere.

RESISTING THE POPULARITY OF GUILT

Make no mistake: To begin releasing your guilt is to go against the way of the world. Many people believe that releasing guilt means condoning errors and abdicating responsibility. But true responsibility inspires a response, an act of change. Guilt points toward a problem while denigrating the abilities of everyone concerned to do anything about it.

To release guilt is not to say, "I didn't do it!" and attempt to shift responsibility elsewhere. To release guilt is to say, "I have done the best I could, and I will try to change or improve to correct my flaws or failures." To release guilt is to surrender our taste for self-punishment. This is revolutionary work, for the world runs on guilt and punishment.

To gauge the popularity of guilt, ask the people you know whether they believe in the effectiveness of punishment. Very few, if any, will answer that they find no use for it at all. What would become of the world, they may ask, without guilt and punishment?

The answer is that the world could become a place of faith and continuous learning. To test this vision, begin answering your own mistakes with an honest, open compassion and the willingness to learn. Never consider the struggle to change yourself a failure; consider it always a learning process whose duration and final outcome are unknown to you. Guilt will tell you that the battle to improve yourself is lost. Responsibility knows that the process of growth is always beginning.

As you learn to treat yourself with kindness, clarity, and responsibility, your own belief in guilt and punishment will subside. Resisting the popularity of guilt begins with casting your single vote for healing instead. It doesn't matter that you will be outnumbered at first, for you are casting your lot with a great power.

RELEASING GUILTY SECRETS

Guilt thrives in secrecy. For many of us, whatever public shame we have suffered pales beside the intensity of private self-condemnation over certain secrets, large or small, that help define our personalities. The first step to releasing any guilty secret is to examine it honestly in a way that is new to most of us. Ask yourself: "How useful is this secret in achieving my ultimate goals in life?" or "What does this secret serve?"

A guilty secret cannot really be released until it is seen as useless to the pursuit of spiritual growth—and spiritual growth is understood to be the process that achieves all of one's important goals. From this point of view, protecting a guilty secret is not "bad" so much as it is a waste of precious and limited time. At the heart of faith is just such a clear and simple practicality.

Of course, the release of profound secrets requires a profound vulnerability: a willingness to be seen for who you truly are, within and without. But I doubt that anyone can surrender all their secrets at once. Indeed, we must start surrendering some of our smaller secrets in order to discover or comprehend our larger secrets. By learning in small steps that the practice of openness and vulnerability leads to freedom, you can eventually develop enough faith to pursue the great freedom of profound vulnerability.

GUILT AND ADDICTION

Although some addictions can entrap the body, they are not the body's fault to begin with. The appetite behind them is the mind's appetite, not the body's, and it is primarily an appetite for guilt. We accept guilt as "natural," and we seek a constant infusion of it to maintain our sense of the normal. What guilt creates is a false sense of stability—an internal condition akin to perpetual crisis management. This is the state of existence most of us are used to.

To constantly feed our minds with guilt, we must do something guilt-inducing. In terms of addiction, we may take something pleasant—for a mild example, let's use a chocolate chip cookie—and we use it as a means to create pain through the repetitive indulgence of remembered pleasure. That is, when we eat something that we remember as pleasurable—but for which we have no hunger— we set ourselves up for the pain of shame ("I have no control"), the pain of self-resentment ("I knew I shouldn't have eaten that cookie"), and the pain of indigestion ("Bleah!"). I know this cycle well, and from my studies I recognize it as the same cycle behind more serious addictions. Serious addictions allow people less time to figure them out before irretrievable damage may be done.

At any rate, when pain and pleasure get mixed up in our minds, they become useless as signals about how to use our bodies wisely in the world. Yet in the confusion of addiction, the mind is not a slave to the body, but a slave to itself. It's the habitual desire for guilt that creates false appetites, and then those appetites get blamed on the poor unsuspecting body. When the body subsequently becomes habituated to particular substances or activities, its urges can seem to be leading us astray—when in fact the body has only done our guilty bidding.

The cure? A simple if challenging moment of awareness with the arising of every addictive urge. Confronting the chocolate chip cookie, cigarette, or drug that looks so good but is not needed, one can ask, "Am I serving my happiness and freedom with this indulgence, or my guilt and enslavement?" That may seem like a big question to ask about a small decision of the moment. But if a small decision is fraught with tension and suffering, then big questions need to be asked. (With profound addictions, medically supervised withdrawal or recovery programs may be necessary before such a question can even be brought to one's awareness.)

This conscious approach to addiction is not an argument against pleasure. Rather it is an argument for the choice of pure and unmitigated pleasure whenever possible, and the denial of pleasure contaminated by guilt. For the fact is that a "guilty pleasure" is no pleasure at all over the long term. It is another surrender to the mind's circular trap of addiction to guilt.

A pure and unmitigated pleasure, by the way, will be some form of authentic service to self or others, or a form of worship. A pure and unmitigated pleasure may be tiny (a chocolate chip cookie enjoyed without guilt) or immense. An immense, pure, and unmitigated pleasure is one type of transcendental experience (see step IV on page xix).

ADDICTION AND FORGIVENESS

We may sometimes realize that an indulgence serves only our guilt and enslavement, and then go ahead with it anyway. These failures to choose freedom must be accepted with as much awareness and forgiveness as we can muster. Forgiveness is the only quality that enables us to succeed after a thousand failures—and the only quality that enables us to grow a little even while we are failing. After all, we learn to accept peace and freedom in tiny increments, and sometimes we have to take two and a half steps back for every three forward.

———

Forgiveness is the only quality that
enables us to succeed after
a thousand failures

———

Rapid change may seem to happen in dramatic moments of crisis and surrender, but such "accelerated" change relies on a lot of preparation (whether we know we have been preparing for change or not). Then, dramatic change needs to be confirmed by months and years of testing, checking, and certifying that one's way of living is really better than it used to be. This is the science of spiritual development.

The acceptance of the real and free self follows the release of guilt. As we gradually give up the chaos of guilt, we slowly find our footing upon the bedrock stability of fearless love. This stability is founded neither on the rigid denial of pleasure nor the slavish avoidance of pain, but on acceptance of both kinds of experience as the natural warp and weft of living in the body. It is in this stable state of mind that we can wisely use pain and pleasure as signals of which way to go and what to do in this world.

ACCEPTING THE LOSS OF GUILT

As an addiction or some other pattern of guilt begins to disintegrate, one may feel a distinct sense of loss. I've confronted this feeling a number of times: "Without this familiar habit, worry, or guilt, who will I be from now on?" As something fixed, heavy, and negative within the self dissolves, an unfamiliar sensation of openness, light, and permeability fills in. Such a change may bring about a feeling of queasiness, but that passes as one's sense of self eventually restabilizes—with more energy, optimism, and flexibility than before.

Everything false and heavy within us is tied to guilt; everything true and light is illuminated by faith.

Accepting the loss of guilt brings on a fundamental realization about the nature of the self. Everything false and heavy within us is tied to guilt; everything true and light is illuminated by faith. Our personalities are limited and deformed by our wounds and guilt. We may take great pride in some of our scars, even defending them to the death against a healing that would dissolve them. To release guilt is to surrender our limitations, and open ourselves to a creativity, generosity, and wisdom that before was unimaginable.

Paradoxically, we become truer to ourselves as we become less defined by our personalities. Along the way there will be many opportunities to mourn the passing of former selves, each of whom were limited by various pretensions and self-deceptions that are no more. It is all right to feel this grief, and proper to honor the person we were yesterday—the person who did the best that he or she could, and by so doing, eventually transcended an old guilt and brought more faith into the world.

GUILT VS. THE NEW MOMENT

We are often so fixed on the past that we overlook the potential of the present. We have never known as much as we do right now; we have a new sum total of knowledge and capacities at every new moment. Thus we are capable of some degree of change at any time, capable of putting together everything we have experienced into a novel awareness of ourselves and the world around us. And we are capable of acting on our novel awareness in unprecedented ways, initiating the liberation of ourselves and others from the dull habits of the past.

Guilt recognizes none of this, and would rather have us believe that a greater darkness is always closing in upon us. The chains that bind us to the habits of the past are forged with guilt. If we do not change, it is because we still believe we are undeserving of the gifts of our own potential.

DARKNESS AND LIGHT

Guilt is darkness, faith is the light; where they coexist is a world of shadows, that is, our world. The body is shadow; the earth is shadow; all matter is shadow. The key to seeing through all of it is the release of guilt. This way the world gradually lightens, and our passage through it becomes less painful.

II

Gathering Trust

Gathering trust is necessary for a spiritual faith to be more than a pretense or naive fantasy. Faith grows from daily acts and decisions of trust—islands of clarity, peacefulness, and responsibility in this world of chaos.

The capacity for trust rests chiefly on one's own trustworthiness; it is far easier to find reasons to trust others when you have every reason to trust yourself. Thus, the key to gathering trust is one's own commitment to truthfulness and personal honor, a commitment necessarily leavened with compassion for human frailty and forgiveness of the human tendency to fail.

Strengthening one's own honor and truthfulness, in a world shot through with illusions and deceptions, is the first faith-building step that is tinged with transcendence. To be trustworthy is to go against the grain of a cynical culture, and some would say, against human nature itself. Thus, to extend trust from the foundation of personal honor is to foster a vision of a new human nature.

God is, in fact, the idea of infinite
and unconditional love.

The work of becoming more trustworthy cannot rely solely on moral campaigns for self-improvement, although they are necessary at times. Rather the work must be fundamentally inspired by recognizing that we are absolutely accepted by God. Only God loves unconditionally, for God originates in a reality without conditions, contradictions, or incompleteness. God is, in fact, the idea of infinite and unconditional love.

To begin accepting God's infinite love is to begin making our own reality less conflicted, more sensible and dependable, more whole and reassuring. Feeling the acceptance of God take root within enables us to become more trustworthy because we directly experience the rewards of serving truth and reliability: we feel smarter, sharper, more peaceful and forgiving.

By contrast, merely telling ourselves to be good engenders tension and inner conflict. It lacks foundation or substance. Believing in goodness is no good without accepting the total, patient love of God.

To accept the love of God, begin to imagine it: perfect acceptance and support without judgment, and an infinite wisdom that corrects with compassion, not condemnation. What you will seem to be imagining is actually the recollected memory of divine affection. Then imagine that great affection entering and opening your heart. When this act of imagination—this mystical memory— begins to yield feelings of release, gratitude, and wonder, then the spiritual work of gathering trust is well under way.

Gathering trust, then, begins with the remembrance of God. Because our world is ruled by forgetfulness—an agonizing loss of memory about our Source—the remembrance of God is a revolutionary act. And the gathering of trust is a continuous uprising against the world's belief in loss and abandonment.

TRUST AND SKEPTICISM

The silent partner of trust is skepticism. This partnership is not as paradoxical as it may sound at first. Because people perpetuate countless illusions upon themselves and others, a trusting vision must be sharp and discerning, for there is no use in trusting illusions as reality. (You can, however, trust illusions as illusions.) What a healthy skepticism contributes to faith is a sense of intuitive direction and wise choice.

Skepticism pursued for its own sake, however, will run amok and mutate into a cynical outlook on life. This outlook actually retards the maturing of trust and replaces faith with a bitter shadow of itself. Unfortunately, self-serving skepticism is far more prominent these days than skepticism in its right proportion, yoked firmly to the service of trust.

The role of skepticism is not to condemn that which is found to be untrustworthy, but to clarify one's appreciation of what is real and genuinely useful. My experience as an investigative reporter taught me that when skepticism becomes tiring and feels like a drag on the spirit, then it has gotten out of proportion and should be reined in. It is tempting to regard this "skepticism fatigue" as a justified world-weariness, the unavoidable burden of looking upon a landscape of misery and wrongdoing. (This is an occupational hazard for cops and reporters.) But faith uses skepticism only to correctly identify the world's problems—and then it looks upon those problems with mercy, and the readiness to ask for divine assistance.

The highest use of skepticism is to question the very reality of the world, to ask if this is how God intended things to be. If we suspect that God did not intend our reality, then we may rightly suspect its authenticity. If this life is but a dream, a keen-eyed faith is the way to our awakening.

TRUST VS. WORRY

Gathering trust requires the willingness to give up worrying. This is a discipline that can perhaps never be entirely mastered, but its effects are cumulative and can make a dramatic difference in one's life.

I worry about ninety percent less than I used to, and I trust people, fate, and the world of our existence that much more. By progressively surrendering the habit of worry I have gained a much greater peace than I used to think possible. And the potential for less worry and still greater peace seems limitless. I have learned to ask myself, whenever

I find myself slipping into worry, "Will this anxiety actually solve the problem at hand?" Invariably, the answer is no. What will solve the problem are attention and creativity, both of which work best in the absence of anxiety. Since I know that high-quality attention and creativity come from deep within—from a mystical source greater than my ordinary self—then I can use worry as a signal that I am trying to trust only myself when I need to trust a greater resource.

To gather trust within oneself is
to sow peace in the world at large.

To release worry is to say, "I recognize that I cannot solve the problem at hand by myself. I commit the problem to God, to all the creative resources within that are beyond my comprehension." And then it is time to wait, quietly, respectfully, and with keen alertness. When one's inner resources offer up a solution to the problem at hand, the creative work can begin. This work will constructively use the energy that worry would otherwise have wasted.

Wherever worry can be challenged and its energy redirected in this way, the seeds of trust can be planted. It is a momentous process whose difficulty is matched only by the wonders of its gains. To gather trust within oneself is to sow peace in the world at large.

RELEASING WORRY
THROUGH FORGIVENESS

We all tend to pick a favorite target for our biggest worry. It's the one person or phenomenon that obviously can't be trusted, and therefore must be anxiously turned over and over in our minds, regardless of whether that process yields any useful results (which it generally doesn't). I suppose many people worry the most about particular relationships, because they have the greatest difficulty learning to trust certain other individuals.

A major worry of my adult life has been about money. Only recently have I realized that finding a way to trust money is a struggle to trust people in the abstract: as a society, a culture, a civilization. Nowadays I see money as a medium of respect and communication. How we hold it, hoard it, use it, or waste it reflects what we are saying to each other—as individuals, groups, organizations, and nations—about how deserving of continued existence and support we believe each other to be. Considering what goes on with money these days, mutual respect seems to be in short supply among human beings.

The inequities of our monetary system are the undeniable expressions of our collective fear about survival and our alienation from each other. Through the confrontation and negotiation of recurring worry about money, I have learned that it's necessary to forgive the lunacy of our monetary system in order to live sensibly within it.

To forgive, it is necessary to get up close to the object of one's fear, sorrow, or resentment. Once when I was quite ill and financially desperate, I fell into a delirious half-sleep where I saw my fear about money in the form of an enormous, scowling stone face—a graven image in the middle of a dark jungle. At a certain distance its visage and presence were terrifying. But in my anxious reverie I saw myself crossing the clearing in front of this harsh god, finally coming up so close to it that the lines of its face were just intriguing designs in a wall of rock. Then I realized that I could get footholds and handholds in the indentations of this wall, and climb it. After an arduous trek upward, I pulled myself over the top of the wall and discovered, much to my surprise, a vast, sunny meadow that afforded me feelings of abundance and well-being.

This vision was an authentic miracle of my inner life—the first time I had sensed the possibility of healing a major wound in my psyche, and of transforming a paralyzing fear. I can't say that a big check arrived the next day, or that my financial situation significantly improved over the next few months. But from that day forward I began suffering less within myself, regardless of my financial circumstances. My vision, creativity, and resourcefulness began improving as a result, eventually pulling me from the depths of financial crisis.

During the dark days of my money troubles, I believed that too much of it went to the wrong places for all the wrong reasons, and that I was only one victim of the system, among many. I still believe the system is insane; there is too much evidence not to think otherwise. This seems to me a proper use of skepticism, and it has saved me more than once from investing in wild schemes promising financial redemption through ungrounded spiritual idealism about the possibilities of money.

But our crazy monetary system has one less victim now—because I have inwardly ceased my own victimization about money. I see it as neither evil nor divine, and thus neither to be avoided nor hoarded.

I am personally dedicated to improving my ways of using and communicating with money, and I am politically committed to seeing that we all learn to improve our communication with it, in order to balance our traditional notions of fiscal responsibility with a broader sense of social responsibility.

———

To trust the world, you must trust yourself first;
to trust yourself, you must be willing
to forgive the unforgivable.

———

What I learned through a years-long struggle with the "almighty dollar bill" was an invaluable lesson about ending worry and gathering trust: To trust the world, you must trust yourself first; to trust yourself, you must be willing to forgive the unforgivable. Anything that seems unforgivable is an angry god within you, even if it seems to be outside you. To overcome an angry god within, it may be necessary to climb the stone face of fear.

TRUST AND THE COUNTING OF BLESSINGS

Trust is appreciation extended toward the future. As such, the energy of trust derives from one's reservoir of appreciation for the present. He who finds few blessings to count in the here-and-now will have a devilishly difficult time trusting the unpredictable future. When you cannot count many blessings, you will count on your narrow expectations to a risky degree.

People and events are unpredictable not because they are inherently unreliable, but because we live in the midst of great mystery. When we decide we can order mystery to suit our plans and purposes, we are setting ourselves up for surprise and betrayal. When we accept a spiritual sense of self arising from an appreciation of the mystery of reality, we can respond to life's twists and turns with an agile adaptability, blaming no one for our disappointments and finding potential in every catastrophe.

Practicing appreciation means counting blessings on a regular basis. For years I have done this at the end of the day, reviewing the day's events and encounters in an appreciative light. Sometimes my appreciation is necessarily rueful, but I search nonetheless for what I have learned from disappointing turns of fate. I follow this ritual not to "be good" but to increase the potency and skillfulness of my trust—for a skillful trust is a great power.

A warning: The ritual of counting blessings (or any other prayer or meditation) that degrades into a pretense of goodness should be abandoned. A practical faith should always be focused on results, even if some of its results can be perceived only in the long term. But a lifeless religious routine can be harmful to the practitioner, and it encourages cynicism among observers who correctly perceive its fruitlessness.

PREPARING FOR THE BEST

It is possible to have mistaken expectations, but it is impossible to be "too trusting." Real trust is deepened and informed by disappointment, just as spiritual vision is refined by disillusionment. Trust prepares us for the best by teaching us to prepare for a future far better than what we may merely hope for.

BETRAYAL AND TRUST

What can be done when we are openly and deliberately betrayed? Isn't betrayal a reason to withdraw our trust from other people and from the world in general? Aren't the bitterest people those who have been most betrayed?

Actually, the bitterest people are those who have the least faith in their own capacity to heal, to change, and to grow. Bitterness arises from the realization that the world has defeated one's hopes or expectations, but bitterness thrives on the belief that no comfort or solution for one's original hurt can ever be found. Some people waste a lot of time waiting bitterly for the past to correct itself, which will never happen.

Thus, the bitter person clings to the murky romance of living in defeat. This is an act of self-hatred that the bitter person may actually believe to be some kind of revenge on the past. Believing that you can avenge the past is primarily an avoidance of growing up. To grow up, one must release self-hatred by saying, "I do not know enough to judge anyone, including myself."

TRUSTING SELF AND OTHERS

It is always true but not always evident: We trust one another exactly to the extent to which we trust ourselves. Here is an extreme example: A thug accosts you in the street, demanding money at gunpoint. Can you trust him? Apparently not.

But what if you could trust yourself to grasp his motivation and desperation so quickly, clearly, and completely that you could disarm him with just words? What if you perceived his attack as a cry for help, and you knew exactly what to do about it in order to save both of you? If you could trust yourself to this extraordinary extent, then you could trust your attacker to be harmless.

I doubt if I could do this—but by no means should this capacity be beyond the pale of possibility. I think it's the capacity we need to be imagining and striving for, in place of our current desire for ever greater vengeance against those who hurt us. And I suspect that the fastest route to this positive capacity is not training in verbal self-defense or negotiating strategies, but in learning to recognize, acknowledge, and surrender the cruel inward attacks we make upon ourselves every day. If we are often holding our own heart at gunpoint, then our spirit withers and our distrust of others grows apace. If we don't learn to take care of our inner thugs—by carefully asking them what they need and firmly explaining that their needs must be peacefully served without harm to others—then we will never understand how to deal effectively with the thugs on the street. We will then have to commit more and more resources to the vain attempt to "lock 'em all up"— simultaneously thickening the walls of our soul's prison at the same time.

UNDERSTANDING OUR SHADOWS

I'm always amused when people refer to the vicious killers among us as "animals." That strikes me as an insult to animals. After all, they don't kill for kicks, or in the name of God, or because their parents abused them. We should say of a vicious killer, "What a human!" Our peculiar viciousness as a species is a potential that lies within our consciousness, and we all have that capacity. We also share the potential for a kind and pragmatic understanding of ourselves as individuals and as a species.

Does that mean that the safety of the human community relies upon our comprehending the depths of the human condition? Yes. Either that, or continue to live partial, fearful, and guarded lives. The real question is whether we have anything more important to do than to pursue a deep and pragmatic understanding of our shadows and light.

Pursuing this knowledge need not displace life's other challenges and tasks. In fact, this pursuit needs to be woven into the fabric of everyday life. If we look upon other people's violence as only their failing—and not our responsibility to heal as a community and a species—we will continue to descend into a spiral of viciousness.

THE OWNERSHIP OF TRUST

We do not create or own our trust, although it is an inborn capacity. To the extent that we gather and practice trust, we learn the relationship of the divine world to our world. Trust is what God gives completely. The fact that we can either give or withhold trust is proof that we have been entrusted with a divine skill to do with as we will. God gives us a chance to be like or unlike God, trusting us to learn, over time, which way of being works better.

TRUST OVER TIME

Like all other spiritual skills, trust is deepened and focused over time. Its potential need will never be frozen as long as we are consciously working to be free of resentments rooted in the past. At times we may trust immaturely—that is, expect people to do things they are not yet capable of—or needlessly withhold our trust. But every misstep or stumble can still carry us forward if we are dedicated to growing our trust with what we have learned.

Authentic service is service to all,
and the development of trust over time
leads us into a full-service life.

To trust one's growth requires a progressively greater surrender to one's inner teacher, a guidance both practical and divine. We can tell when the guidance is genuine rather than delusionary because real guidance will always be altruistic and calming, even if it directs us to do unusual or daring things. Over time, this guidance will help us see that altruism is also self-serving. Authentic service is service to all, and the development of trust over time leads us into a full-service life.

In another light, the process of gathering trust is a negotiation with God about how much doubt and self-defense we will yield for the sake of peace and goodwill to all of creation. In the end, we will give everything away willingly. What we learn from a growing trust is exactly why we want to do that.

III

Practicing Patience

A spiritual faith often requires a special kind of waiting—not a fidgety, toe-tapping, clock-watching kind of waiting, but a restful waiting, a secure expectation. Patience is the practice of abiding, and one abides in one's abode. It's the kind of waiting that can happen only when one feels at home.

Home, in a spiritual sense, is an inner realm ruled by an astute self-acceptance and a wise fondness for the world at large. In this home there is always a good telescope at the windows, its optics lovingly maintained, pointed up toward the ever-changing face of Creation. Around this home there are acres of rolling meadows yielding to limitless expanses of wild forest, mountains, and sea.

To wait patiently for anything or anyone is to remember that we can always sit by the window or on the porch of our inner home and experience the timelessness of the spirit, like a breeze that blows through our open windows carrying the news from the great beyond. If anyone tells you to "be patient," you can repeat it to yourself as, "Be at home." When patience is called for, retreat to the inner, stable center where you can abide.

Patience is deciding in favor of attention rather than tension.

Patience is an instinct we all carry within us, for it is the human experience of nature's timing. The rose unfolds patiently; a tree grows old and great the same way. Of course we may forget the instinct of patience as easily, and as painfully, as we forget nature's abiding within us. What we choose to believe about ourselves, what we pretend is important, is what sends us rushing against the clock in a senseless way. What we remember of our true nature—what remains magnificent within us—gives us the capacity to live without fear of time.

Patience is deciding in favor of attention rather than tension. Attending to the inner part of ourselves that knows timelessness, we can wait in the world of time and balance our hurried sense of self-interest with the timeless knowledge that all will be well—even when the "all" swallows us, as it inevitably will. Patience, then, is also humility, a surrender to the transcendent. Patience is the rhythm of faith.

HOW TO PRACTICE PATIENCE

Be compassionate to your impatience. This is not the same as doing its bidding or believing everything it tells you. Instead, accept that impatience signals an inner belief that you are somehow being cheated, insulted, forgotten, or ignored—by others, by God, or by yourself.

In any case, implementing compassion for your impatience means choosing the most productive route toward whatever you are waiting for. This entails asking what you are really waiting for, in the biggest possible sense, even if your impatience of the moment is about something petty. (But if you are impatient for something petty, why waste the precious energy of your awareness on something unimportant?) Rather than chafing perpetually against the delay of what you want, you can give yourself the inner comfort of a secure expectation that what you truly need will eventually be delivered—and that whatever you expect but don't need will eventually fall out of your awareness.

If you are impatient for something large and important, like justice for all, then you need to choose the most effective state of mind on which to base your actions. Acting on a righteous impatience sometimes gets results, but there is always some war created around the edges. A righteous patience derives from a clearer vision that is merciful towards all, even the perceived perpetrators of insult and injustice. A righteous patience brings unseen powers to bear on your situation, because it is a state of mind aligned with your inborn spiritual purpose. This state of mind might also be called sublime confidence—a confidence not that your little self will be served in all its chaotic, shifting aims, but that the greater good of all will be served by your acceptance of deep guidance.

Therefore, to practice patience is to use your impatience as a signal to call on greater powers. Whether you are stuck in a traffic jam or waiting for world peace, replace the anxious queries of "When?" and "How much longer?" with the reassurances, "God is with me" or "Whatever else I may feel, there is also a great peace within me always." That's how to cease waiting on events in time and transport yourself into timeless contemplation.

This is not to say that one can or should disconnect from the world's problems or concerns. In fact, everyone is capable of timeless contemplation while attending effectively to the situation at hand. For the key to faith and equanimity is a constant awareness of two worlds of experience. If we are completely absorbed by the timed, material world, then our lives will tend to be mean and dispirited. If we are completely absorbed by the timeless spiritual world, we cannot function effectively in an everyday world that needs our contributions.

THE FINEST IMPATIENCE

Patience is waiting with intention. The finest kind of patience carries the intention of love. Intending to love, we may sometimes fall short, and become impatient; but even so we can say that the intention of love is behind the finest kind of impatience.

PATIENCE VS. PASSIVITY

Because patience has an intent, it should not be confused with an unhealthy passivity, that is, waiting around for something good to happen because we do not want to work for change.

If you want to get struck by lightning, you can't do it by curling up on the couch under a warm blanket in the safety of your own house while a storm rages outside. Rather you have to be willing to run into an open field in the middle of the storm, and then wait out there, soaked and shivering . . . and then it still may not happen.

But who wants to get struck by lightning anyway? The lightning that's worth waiting (and shivering) for is *enlightenment*, a shocking moment of growth in which some habitual, fearful part of oneself gets burned away and something new, pure, and child-like emerges to refresh and renew one's way of life. In various traditions, such a shock is also called *kensho*, or self-realization, or the holy instant.

The bolt of enlightenment seldom strikes the passive—those attempting to sleep through life and only grumble and turn over on the couch when prodded to awaken. This kind of lightning does eventually strike the patient. It hits those who have ventured bravely into storm after storm of self-confrontation and waited studiously, their faces upturned to the rain and the roiling clouds. The irony is that when lightning does strike the patient seeker, it usually happens when least expected—like a bolt from the blue, as the old saying goes.

Once it has been received by someone willing, this kind of lightning can find the same target again and again in a single life-time. Enlightenment strikes many times before the burning it gives is complete.

DISCIPLINE, WILL, AND PATIENCE

I've had a struggle with discipline all of my life, torn between an attraction to rigorous physical or mental regimens and an equally powerful yearning to relax, to be self-satisfied without having to self-correct, to let come what may. Although I began working at a young age with disciplines like yoga and meditation (beginning the latter before I even knew what I was doing), I never applied myself consistently or for very long periods before forgetting my routines and becoming distracted by other concerns. And then I would berate myself for being impatient and lacking "willpower."

Now that I have learned to maintain several steady if not rigid disciplines, I realize that I used to have the means and ends all mixed up. Patience and a reliable will are what you learn by taking up disciplines, failing with them, and starting them over again, refining your direction and intensity at every step. Whatever else a discipline may promise—a clear mind, a lithe body, some well-honed skill—is actually secondary to the development of one's faithfulness, the slowly-gathered will and patience to refocus the mind in order to suffer less and become more useful.

We are always changing the world. In the midst of our pains, distractions, and forgetfulness it is easy for us to create negative change through mistakes, ill will, or negligence. Thus, any noticeable improvement in this world is no accident. Someone with transformative discipline will have been on the scene recently.

WAITING ON NOTHING

What I once thought I knew about patience was nothing compared to what I learned in the experience of total defeat brought about by a prolonged illness. The peculiar nature of my disease seemed custom-designed for the teaching of patience, for I had to spend long periods of time in considerable pain and exhaustion, barely functioning, without noticeably improving or getting any worse. For the greater part of three years I lived in a chaotic and disheartening limbo, unable to prepare for the return of health but certain that I was not facing death either. Improvements and relapses occurred in such nonsensical patterns that I could never be sure of whether my medicines, attitude adjustments, and hard-bargained life changes were helping me or not.

Until I became ill, I had always missed the presence of a single great teacher in my life, someone whose power and wisdom would be so great and obvious that I could openly submit myself to that teacher's will. My devotional drive had always been effectively countered by a sharp eye for human frailties; I was not about to be taken in by some crackpot guru. So life sent me a great but invisible teacher who would prove more cruel, irrational, and ultimately instructive than any guru I had ever heard of. This crackpot guru lived in my own veins and tissues, and I unwittingly invited him in with my bitterness and faithlessness. Once inside me, he would not be dislodged by mere plaints, prayers, or pills.

When you learn to wait patiently on nothing,
your inner teacher can begin to arrange your real life.

So I learned to wait—through storms and tortures, through bedridden boredom and wild lonesomeness, past all reason or sensible expectations. I learned to wait on nothing because everything seemed lost. And then, as I fitfully began to recover, miraculous things happened that I could never have imagined, that certainly weren't on any of my old schedules, and that would direct my life on a new and unexpected path.

When you learn to wait patiently on nothing, your inner teacher can begin to arrange your real life, working noiselessly and invisibly behind the screen of apparent reality, deftly moving people, signs, and circumstances into open view at just the right time for you to recognize them as accelerators of your new and yet ancient purpose. No doubt there are easier ways to learn this kind of mystical, transformative waiting than being taught patience by defeat. Defeat just happened to be my teacher, a better and more exhaustive teacher than I could have sought out consciously.

So I know what happens when Godot arrives. He brings an end to aimlessness, and he brooks no compromise.

THE RIVER OF POSSIBILITIES

Patience recognizes that there is always a much greater range of possibilities at hand than the limited outcomes we can plan, predict, or produce. Impatience awaits something in particular; patience expects the continuous flow of the unexpected. To be patient about the sights and sounds ahead on a journey down the river, imagine the point of view of the river.

WAITING ON THE WORLD TO CHANGE

I used to be more aggravated with the world, and more impatient for momentous social changes to come about quickly. I was focused on political aims and reform, and saw anyone with differing politics as obstacles to the changes that anyone in their right mind— my mind, that is—should desire. Thus my approach to world-changing was plugged into the oppositional tug-of-war that has always characterized political struggle.

It's probably fortunate that I had lit-tle or no influence during the years that I believed in struggle and opposition. I was actually too self-absorbed to have much effect beyond my immediate concerns and relationships, and I maintained a personal complacency that was actually antithetical to change. By age thirty, I had decided there was little possibility of altering my fundamental assumptions and ways of relating. After all, I reasoned, I was an adult, and whoever I had become by that age was who I was likely to remain.

Being on a spiritual path means accepting citizenship in a world of ongoing transformation.

It would take me a while to realize that my impotent anxiousness for the world to change arose primarily from my refusal to change myself. All this is different for me now. Being on a spiritual path means accepting citizenship in a world of ongoing transformation. With experience, it becomes increasingly difficult—and unimportant—to distinguish one's inner world from the outer, or the observer from the observed. A spiritual perspective is constantly expanding beyond the individual's narrowly focused needs and prejudices. This perspective actually engenders more direct and effective responses to the world's problems than the oppositional politics of the ego.

One should keep in mind, however, that a spiritual response doesn't always operate in visible realms, and so its effect cannot always be quantified.

But in general it can be said that a spiritual politics demonstrates the qualities of humility, charity, and ever-widening attentiveness—which compare well to the ego's conventional politics of arrogance, suspicion, and one-track stubbornness. Above all, a spiritual politics demonstrates a caring patience, founded in the awareness that the world, like the individual, seldom changes for the better as quickly as we would like. In both cases the same difficulty may be at hand—for how we see the world has a great deal to do with our inner difficulties.

In my own case, I have missed far too many of my private deadlines for change ever to lay another judgment on other people, cultures, nations, or the world at large for not changing fast enough. I don't know how much can be changed or how quickly the world's great pain can be eased, but I am now certain that patience increases possibilities and reduces suffering. For me, waiting on the world to change means making the best possible use of my own time.

PATIENCE, GENTLENESS, AND SUBTLETY

The politics of a practical faith might best be described as "patience within, gentleness without." As a pioneering, bulldozing culture we are used to equating strength with force—especially violent force—and so we are slow to recognize the subtler strengths of patience and gentleness. But it has been observed by many that it is the gentle warrior who wins without a fight; it has even been rumored that the meek shall inherit the earth. If the future is already in their hands, then the meek—who are also the patient, the gentle, and the subtle—must be more powerful than we have imagined.

IV

Learning Transcendence

Transcendence is a big word that does not get much respect in our culture. Translated from the Latin root, it means "to climb over." I like that root definition; it clearly implies the work required to progress from a narrow or ordinary state of mind to a bigger, more inclusive state. One doesn't simply float into enlightenment, or compassion, or faith. When one suddenly experiences a transcendent moment, it's like coming to the top of a mountain. The complete vista may not be in view until the last step, and thus it may seem that one movement was all it took to get there. In the ecstasy and wonderment of the Big View, one may be tempted to forget all the time spent setting up base camp, trudging patiently over miles of stony trails, and hanging on for dear life to sheer rock faces. One has to labor for liberation. But it's liberation that finally gives meaning to the toil it takes to get there.

Faith is always headed in a transcendent direction. And faith is, among other things, the attempt to hold inside ourselves the feeling of transcendence—a mysterious knowledge of the infinity, grandeur, and magnificence that are all around us every day, but are so often forgotten. In this aspect, a spiritual faith is applied awe.

This part of faith feels illogical because our minds cannot grasp infinity; the most we can hold of it is a passing, translucent sensation of sublimity. The greatest faith we can hold onto is the tiniest particle of an overwhelming truth, yet that particle has a nourishing radioactivity. It ameliorates the ever-present sorrow of life on this earth with the ever-glowing tranquility of the life beyond. Without a particle of transcendent faith, life is dry and dispirited, an aching slavery to the treadmill of survival.

Our culture is embarrassed, ignorant, and fearful of transcendence, often to the point of calling it madness. Yet we see all around us the innate, desperate urge to transcend ourselves through negative means such as alcoholism, drug addiction, sex addiction, shopping addiction, fame, wealth, and power addictions, and so on. In love with our rational, scientific, and deadly dull view of what constitutes reality, we have devised an awkward strategy to deal with our instinctive transcendent urges: First we ridicule or demonize transcendent experience; then we build an economy—both lawful and illicit—that caters inappropriately to our frustrated yearnings for transcendence; then we tell our kids to "just say no" to the whole idea. And we wonder why our culture seems to be going nuts!

In indigenous, so-called "primitive" cultures still animated by an instinctive spirituality, it is accepted that transcendent experience helps people understand their purpose in the human community. This is what initiation rituals are for; at their best they help young people get a practical view of what their life on earth is supposed to be about. That practical view is a kind of triangulation, whose three points might be identified as Self, Community, and the Great Beyond. You have to journey into the Great Beyond—and know how to safely return there occasionally—to keep a sane perspective on your everyday life. That's just how it is. Relying on religion to tell us what the Great Beyond is all about won't cut it; we have to have some firsthand experience. Fortunately, access is easier than NASA, our religious leaders, or our greatest scientific minds might believe. The route is through inner space.

The journey into inner space is not always pleasant. I was "initiated" to my purpose in life through a painful crisis, and I didn't care for that experience at the time. But the labor of it liberated me. And now, some years down the road, I'm still relearning what I knew in my childhood, but forgot on the rocky road of adulthood: Transcendence is as near as nature and my own dreams, as readily accessible as looking at the nightly canopy of stars. Transcendence is an inborn capacity to go beyond myself, whenever I am willing to slow down enough to stop worrying about being myself.

Have you ever gazed at a clear sky long enough to realize you are not looking at a huge blue screen, but peering into the infinite? Have you ever watched a large old tree long enough to sense a bit of its incomprehensible might and balance, as it holds up its lengthy limbs toward the warmth of a vastly distant burning star? Have you ever stared at your hand until it seemed a total mystery?

In these and countless other transcendental, easily accessible experiences lies the practical heart of mysticism. Of all the things that our lonely culture is desperately seeking, perhaps it longs to regain a mystical heartbeat most of all. The good news is that we live in the midst of mystery at every moment. *We are mystery*. The scientific notion that we can disassemble and eventually analyze all of nature, and our own consciousness, is ludicrous.

Of all the things that our lonely culture is desperately seeking, perhaps it longs to regain a mystical heartbeat most of all.

To awaken to transcendence is to admit a simple truth: We do not know what is going on—in our cells, in our own minds, in the core of a tree, in the great distances between planets, stars, and galaxies. The paradox is that by giving up trying to analyze and demystify reality all the time, we can find the key to a practical faith, a deep self-realization, and an illimitable joy.

To admit that we are surrounded by mystery is to recognize ourselves. To learn transcendence is to unlearn the miserable notion that we are alone.

FAITH AND LONGING

Inside faith is longing; this is the secret of its energy. This longing is the desire to return to God, to creation itself, to the forgotten state of union we knew before we knew ourselves as individuals. The way back to this union is through longing; *to belong is to be longing*. Without longing, faith is a forced march through the constant doubting of the lonely and imperiled ego. It is self-preservation without sustenance.

Longing is ecstatic and periodically dangerous. Many religions avoid the teaching or practice of longing, and have become tepid as a result. Some religions have not forgotten longing but have tried to civilize it, scheduling it (usually in the form of prayer) into the morning service along with the hymns and the passing of the silver plate. But longing does not respond well to scheduling.

Religious longing draws sensible people into cults, and diverts their natural capacity for faith into the service of wayward teachers and outright maniacs. Our culture is unfamiliar with ecstatic longing and embarrassed by its expressions, so we repress it. Thus, when spiritual longing does erupt in our lives, we can be easily overwhelmed by it, feeling a great liberation in throwing off all logic and skepticism.

But a practical faith holds longing and rationality in balance, like a minister who joins two contrary lovers in a lifetime vow to honor and obey each other. Many people may think it impossible for longing and logic to simultaneously obey each other. Yet it is within that paradoxical fire of opposites that a transcendent and creative clarity is shaped. Between the anvil of longing and the hammer of skepticism we can shape ideas and solutions of profound originality, strength, and durability.

FAITH AND SURRENDER

Faith requires surrender. In the course of a day we may claim so many false and ludicrous victories—we got a parking space, we got a free lunch, we got even with somebody—that a daily, authentic surrender to a bigger reality is hardly excessive.

I try to surrender at the beginning of the day, before I've made any decisions or developed too many anticipations about what should happen in the coming twenty-four hours. I pray simply that I will accept whatever is coming my way in a spirit of gratitude, understanding that what I will believe has happened, good or bad, is only the surface of reality. What seems to be going on is only what I am allowing myself to perceive at any given moment. In other words, reality is always transcendent, whereas I just occasionally get a glimpse of the transcendent.

———

Religious tolerance is the willingness to surrender our various partial ideas of God to the possibility of a uniting, transcendent God

———

The same is true of God. If we're going to "believe" in God, I think we have to believe in a God we don't know very well. Because the God we think we know, based on the religious or cultural ideas most familiar to us, is merely our own partial myth of God. Thus, to believe only in that God is to pray and surrender only to our own ideas. To have faith in a transcendent God is to take a chance on an ultimate and incomprehensible creativity. We can all share equally and fruitfully in that creativity if we are open, patient, and willing to release our guilt in the name of peace.

Religious tolerance is the willingness to surrender our various partial ideas of God to the possibility of a uniting, transcendent God, a God who resolves all paradoxes and dissolves every apparent conflict. If we can surrender our personal expectations for each day to the will of such a God, we may someday be able to surrender our religious conflicts as well.

WHEN TROUBLE IS TRANSCENDENT

An emotional or moral crisis often induces the feeling of being pushed up against a wall, forced beyond our capacities or unfairly intimidated by fate. Perhaps it's tiresome to say that every such challenge represents a kind of opportunity, but in this case the cliché derives from an uncomfortable truth.

This is not to suggest that we should fake a cheery enthusiasm about times when our lives seem to be falling apart. But I would like to suggest that it's important to keep an eye out for the falseness of too much pessimism as well. Pessimism is much more popular in our culture than enthusiasm (which originally meant "inspired by a god"), and so we are seldom skeptical of the authenticity of pessimism, and even more rarely do we question its usefulness.

In dreams I have had the peculiar experience of traveling through walls in order to leave a room. (In a dream this seems like a more direct way to exit than using the door—God only knows why.) This passing through the wall always precipitates a crisis. The passage is difficult and fearful, and I always realize about halfway through that I've undertaken something extraordinary that I don't rationally know how to do. I feel a peculiar but very distinct interchanging of my molecules with the molecules of the wall. My dreambody doesn't punch a hole in the wall and then go through. It mixes with the wall, and while I am in the middle of the transit I feel that I am both the wall and myself, although I also know that I am what is moving through the wall and that the wall is what will stay. When the passage is complete, I invariably find myself floating in the sky, able to fly freely.

When trouble confronts us, we are indeed being pushed up against a wall—but if we turn to face it with an open, exploratory attitude, we may discover that it is not as impenetrable as it first appears. Finding opportunity in crisis means mixing with the crisis, letting our shape match its shape temporarily, letting our particles exchange places with its particles as we push our way through fear and ultimately through the crisis itself. It is a mystical, inexplicable process that is always new in each occurrence of crisis. This means it is an initiation demanding new learning, and offering yet another chance to earn our wings.

DREAMS AND TRANSCENDENCE

Dreams are the perfect teachers of transcendence: regularly available, if a bit challenging to access; intimately personal and creative, yet impossible to claim entirely as products of one's ego; and impenetrable to complete analysis yet capable of changing one's life direction with occasional bursts of ferocious symbolism and feeling. Our culture's general unfamiliarity with the language of dreams is one indicator of our disconnection with instinctive spirituality.

It's no accident that the society that has most devalued dreams has created a colossal motion picture, television, and video industry. The need to experience alternate realities will not be denied. The feverish development of virtual reality technology is an attempt to carry the artificial creation of dreams one step further, but it isn't really necessary. Each of us already has free access to a transcendent realm of alternate realities.

Our dreams know us, often better than we consciously know ourselves.

A friend of mine tells the story of an anthropologist who took a television to an indigenous tribe. Within just a couple of hours, they became disinterested with the tube and returned thereafter to the entertainments of their own storyteller. When the scientist pointed out to one of the villagers that the TV knew many more stories, he replied, "Yes, but the storyteller knows me."

This is precisely the difference between our dreams and movies. Our dreams know us, often better than we consciously know ourselves. A film is deeply affecting when it seems to know us, connecting both intellectually and emotionally in a way that reveals us to ourselves and decreases our sense of isolation. But most film and broadcast media cater chiefly to our desire to be entertained, a healthy motive in the right proportion. However, in a culture where many people live without a sense of purpose beyond mere survival, the motive to be entertained grows all out of proportion, becoming a constant and sometimes desperate addiction to distraction from the aching of one's soul starvation.

Dreams can be as entertaining or uplifting or thrilling or scary as any movie, yet they are always teaching us about us. Often their messages are strictly personal; occasionally they are profoundly instructive about the fundamental nature of consciousness and reality. The most sophisticated understanding of dreams is that they are not all that much different from what we call reality. This is the beginning of transcendent vision.

DEPRESSION, SHADOW, AND TRANSCENDENCE

I grew up on intimate terms with depression, as it haunted my mother's life and I experienced it in both emotional and physiological forms through my first thirty years. Though depression is widely regarded as a psychological or biochemical disorder, I have come to understand it also as a form of spiritual crisis. To me, its growing prevalence in our society is a sign of our spiritual alienation. For what I have to say about it, I can claim no clinical confirmation nor even much agreement from experts in the field. I can say that I have had many opportunities to meet and overcome depression in my own life, and through that process this is what I have learned:

Depression is, according to its degree, the relative absence of a spiritual faith. Severe depression is a negative mystical state in which the sufferer is in danger because the presence of God—as a vital and deeply felt creative force, not merely a religious belief—has been virtually driven from awareness. This is why nothing seems possible. The severely depressed person is limited strictly to the resources of his or her own ego that, without divine energy to draw upon, has no resources. Thus, the depressed person is face to face with the horror of his or her own nothingness. This is the realm of absolute shadow.

Depression is, according to its degree,
the relative absence of a spiritual faith.

The irony of depression is that it teaches one truth: the ego, that self-made idea of ourselves, really is nothing. The more we depend on it alone, the less life force and creative possibility will be available to us. The experience of depression is humiliating, yet the road into depression is paved with hubris— because in one way or another, there has been an increasing exclusion of faith from daily life, and the acceptance in its place of either habitual cynicism or its twin, habitual victimization.

Cynicism masks its arrogance by pretending to be factual and rational. Victimization masks its arrogance by refusing to move beyond the suffering of attack or catastrophe, often proclaiming a false right to vengeance in the process. To collaborate with either of these states is to invite depression; to resist them is to elect faith.

The best thing to do in the midst of depression is to recognize its negative mysticism and respectfully confront the lies it tells. One or more of the following strategies may prove helpful in this regard:

Turn to nature. Depression tends to isolate the individual within his or her own private realm of experience, and then makes that realm seem inescapable. Spending time in nature and paying attention to nature can return a proper perspective to one's inner world.

Activate the body, preferably in a playful way. Depression tends to deny the body's own nature, especially the childlike aspects of that nature. Playing the silliest physical games can help redirect depressive energies. In fact, a sure sign that depression holds sway over one's consciousness is an angry refusal to play.

Confront guilt and other negative convictions. The biggest lie that depression tells is that it is impossible to change one's mind. Whenever I feel the sickly lure of depression, I have learned to think: "I must be wrong about something that I don't have to be wrong about." Usually I discover that I have decided to feel guilty or deeply pessimistic about something that I do not understand sufficiently to judge.

Ask God for help. The big stumbling block for atheists and cynics in depression is that they fear God as a punishing parent, or they resent someone else's overbearing idea of God. But God is Someone who wants only to be of use to anyone in suffering—a mystical partner who responds to a plea as simple and serious as: "I need help from beyond myself." This practical and generous God responds by lifting one's spirits, and doesn't even bill for services rendered. (Anyone who tells you that God does charge for assistance is trying to divert funds for some unwholesome use.)

If we can entertain the possibility that there is a helpful and infinitely resourceful God to call upon in every circumstance, then we can maintain enough humility to make depression the road never chosen. After all, there are better states in which to realize the nothingness of the ego; bliss, for instance. Depression fixates upon the deadly notion "I am nothing." Bliss celebrates the liberating truth "I am nothing without God." In that seemingly simple difference lies the choice between deadening despair and a livable joy.

RENUNCIATION

In a culture that confuses freedom with the unlimited right to self-indulgence, we have a hard time understanding the spiritual value of renunciation. We make the mistake of seeing renunciation as nothing more than self-denial; then we accord self-denial a kind of phony nobility; and then we feel free to admit that we are just not up to being all that noble. If we are in the thrall of these assumptions, then we are likely to live a life devoted mostly to easily gained, short-term gratifications, and end up wondering why we have never experienced a deeper satisfaction.

Properly seen, renunciation is not self-denial at all, but rather an invaluable part of self-transcendence. It's the "climbing over" our own habits and limitations into a fresh and constantly evolving way of being. Of course renunciation is not easy—whether one is renouncing smoking in order to find a fuller breath, or renouncing a Mercedes in order to share the wealth. In fact, it is just too damn difficult to choose against what is delicious, irresistible, and easily grabbed or bought, unless you understand that renunciation benefits you and everyone else more in the long term. To be transformative, renunciation has to be a practical choice, not a religious imperative.

I have never been a great renunciator, but I have practiced enough to learn that a true renunciation delivers a moment of pain. There is a distinct sensation of loss and confusion as the self—who is fond of repeating pleasant or familiar routines—feels the shock of a new direction chosen by the greater Self. This moment of pain should be attended closely and with care, for it can be read as a measurement of one's own readiness for change. A pain that screams in terror may signal that the renunciation being attempted is too great for the present time. A pain that slyly whimpers may signal that the intended renunciation is not quite sincere, or perhaps not as adventurous as it could be.

We may either pity or admire those who choose a renunciate's life in a cloistered environment, but appearances can deceive. Over the long term, such a dramatic renunciation may be easier in a closed culture that demands or reinforces it. It is in the midst of the tempting modern world—free-wheeling, free-spending, and always advertising self-indulgences—that voluntary renunciation may hold the greatest transcendent potential. In the thick of the merry material world, renunciation can be transforming even if practiced in fits and starts.

In other words, renunciation need not be a romantic lunge at purity when a courageous courtship of transcendence will suffice.

DIRECT EXPERIENCE

Most people adopt a religion either because it was handed down to them or because an irreligious way of life proved too dangerous or disheartening to continue. The purpose of most religions is to provide people with a fixed explanation of the mysteries of existence, and a set of moral guidelines by which to live a productive life. As long as religious beliefs are not used as weapons, a conventional religious life can be one of reasonable peacefulness, productivity, and virtue. It is not meant so much to challenge or change one's nature as to control and make the most of it.

A spiritual path, however, is a transformative journey into the transcendent. It begins with the realization that things are not as they seem, and that religious rules about reality are useful only insofar as one accepts the common agreement about what reality is. When you begin to see through "consensus reality" into transcendent realms, it becomes necessary to start exploring the mysteries of existence on your own. Religious ideas become theories to be tested first-hand rather than accepted without question, and the veteran spiritual seeker tests as many kinds of ideas as possible along the way to discovering his or her own unique perspectives on divinity, creation, and human purpose.

A spiritual path, however, is a transformative journey into the transcendent.

In this process, a spiritual path changes one's nature from the inside out; it brings about a real reformation of the individual. As that process deepens, the individual becomes capable of living by his or her own instinctive moral code, a code that surpasses social and religious rules for governing behavior and serving the human community.

We live in a time when more people than ever before are becoming spiritual seekers, true explorers on the path. Whether they seek truth inside or outside churches, mosques, and temples, more and more people are finding it necessary to see through the ordinary circumstances of their lives and glimpse a transcendent reality. Along the way they develop a practical faith in God, or an all-creative wisdom. This God, or wisdom, is directly experienced in these people's spiritual practices.

In the same way that conventional religion has failed many people, conventional politics are failing to keep pace with the demands of a rapidly changing world. The old oppositions of left vs. right, rich vs. poor, and rights vs. responsibility no longer serve, and it is increasingly clear that political leaders and activists must become the ideas they promote. In other words, the politics of the future will belong to transformed individuals who have made change real within themselves before attempting to change the world. In general, the signs of their authenticity will be humility, flexibility, and empathy.

To make change real within ourselves is to embody transcendence—to know God as a transformative force constantly at work within ourselves, rather than merely to believe in God as an external judge or savior. Thus, the politics of the future will be spiritually charged but not religiously prescribed; the politics of the future will be a practical faith in action, instead of a cultural agenda being pursued merely in the name of faith.

THE ARRIVAL OF REVERENCE

Reverence is the recognition of the sublime within the ordinary, a recognition that automatically inspires thanksgiving. Reverence cannot be taught or enforced. Reverence arrives on its own, as the unbidden reward of practicing faith.

———————

Reverence is simultaneously
a gift we realize and an
offering we make.

———————

"Saying grace," for instance, is merely an act without *feeling grace*. We feel grace grow within us as our guilt is released, our trust is strengthened, and our patience is developed. Then, at unpredictable moments, we find ourselves able to touch the transcendental part of our own nature. In recognition of that limitlessness, we begin to understand divinity as something real and life-giving, something at the root of our being and something surrounding our being completely; something we cannot help but revere.

Thus, reverence is simultaneously a gift we realize and an offering we make. Reverence electrifies our consciousness with gratitude for the transcendence we have so far learned.

V

The Rewards
of a Spiritual Faith

There is a part of any spiritual path that is irreducibly mystical—that is, you live the path simply because it irresistibly draws and directs you, and its benefits are felt so deeply that they may be difficult to explain in words. It is important to remember that living in faith can never be wholly defended in conventional terms of profit and loss.

But the seeker who cannot articulate *any* rewards of choosing to live spiritually runs the risks of sinking into lonely delusions, being conned by phony teachers, or resorting to fanaticism in order to shore up beliefs that have failed the test of usefulness. A mystical belief that produces no demonstrable, positive change in one's life is merely spiritual romanticism. By "demonstrable" I mean something that other people notice, or at least an interior change in one's feelings, attitudes and worldview that is so remarkable it results in a sense of wonder, joy, and reverence.

A mystical belief that produces no demonstrable, positive change in one's life is merely spiritual romanticism.

Of course, spiritual romanticism has its charms, and it sells pretty well. Too much contemporary spiritual writing is couched in airy, romantic language that leaves readers with something like a mental sugar high, providing a short-term but ultimately inapplicable kind of inspiration. Knowing how easy it is to slip into spiritual romanticism, I have thought a great deal about the specific improvements that have come about in my life as a result of pursuing a practical faith. In closing I'd like to discuss these rewards in terms as clear and concrete as possible. By doing this I hope to provide readers with definite information on the value of surrendering cynicism, chronic anger, and other self-destructive and fruitless perspectives on life—perspectives that lately are "all the rage," so to speak.

I began this book by saying that a practical faith can supply the experience of stability, security, and fulfillment, qualities that are at the core of what people long for in life. Here is how I understand these qualities:

STABILITY. Maintaining a practical faith at the center of my consciousness means that my worries and doubts cannot live there. Instead they must inhabit the edges of my self-awareness, where they belong. Before the health and spiritual crisis that induced me to regain my instinctive childhood faith, my doubts and worries frequently invaded or even held sway over my "center" all throughout my young adulthood. These anxieties drew off my vital energy and used that energy to distract and misdirect me. As a result, my inner life was chaotic and disheartening. This condition dominated my outer life of work and relationships as well.

Experiencing a stable core of spiritual faith not only drives my problems to the edges of my awareness, but changes my perspective on them as well. Living my faith reminds me that I am always on a path of healing the pain, incompleteness, and isolation of being human. Thus I can regard any problem or challenge that arises in terms of healing.

The questions that I used to ask myself when under pressure—*How could I be so stupid? . . . Why am I being attacked for no reason? . . . Why is life so unfair? . . . What's the use of trying to be or do good?*— are replaced by one inquiry: *How will the problem at hand serve the healing of myself and humanity?* In this way, I experience my problems and resultant worries as my "leading edge" of learning. Instead of serving as proof that there is something wrong with myself or the world, my unresolved concerns serve as directional pointers toward what I have yet to learn.

From day to day, this central core of faith at my center provides me with a mental and emotional stability that compares remarkably well to the instability of my earlier life. Many people grow more stable as they age (and some do not). But I am not talking about the maturing process of a self-serving ego, which often brings a stability rife with bitterness, suspicion, and closed-mindedness. By contrast, I arrived at a stable faith through learning to surrender ego, a process that is apparently never finished in this world but that can nonetheless be pursued with increasing skill and success.

Moving our worries and doubts to the edges of awareness is in fact the same process as removing the fearful, heavily defended ego from the center of our awareness. This allows faith—which, like a seed, is not of our making but can be planted and nurtured with our deliberate care—to root and grow into a great and stable tree at the center of our being.

SECURITY. Stability and security are critically linked because many of the anxieties of insecurity—*"Does anyone love me?"... "Will I have enough money?"... "Am I in danger?"*—are actually symptoms of an inward instability projected onto outer concerns. When very little stability is felt within, the outer world seems terrifying or deliberately vengeful. When self-reliance and trustworthiness are felt within, the outer world is seen more accurately.

Still, a practical faith does not guarantee loving relationships, a good job or income, or safety from all dangers; in fact there are no guarantees of these things because the world is unpredictable, dangerous, and unsecured. Were the world constantly safe, nurturing, and reliable, there would be no need for faith at all. So faith is best seen as the most practical strategy for maximizing our potential to deal with a world where we cannot know what will happen next.

Nonetheless, my practice of faith has delivered many of the elements of security that I used to seek without success. I worry less than I used to about my economic condition, despite the fact that my "bottom line" isn't that much better than it has ever been. And while I exercise reasonable caution on city streets and country trails, I am not pursued by fears of crime, accidents, or persecution. I accept that this is a world in which all kinds of terrible things could happen to me or my loved ones, regardless of my faith. But at least I save myself daily from the punishing anxiety of paranoia. In this way a practical faith supplies much more security than I ever achieved through faithless schemes and self-defensiveness.

How does this work? A spiritual faith supplies a reasonable degree of security because deep within faith there is a mystical knowledge of another world, another realm of existence that is perfectly secure, constant, and unchanging. In religious traditions this faintly recalled otherworld is called "paradise" or Heaven, and is variously believed to precede or follow our existence, to be underneath or far above this world, to be everyone's ultimate destination or a just reward reserved solely for the righteous.

I believe that paradise is, like God, an *idea*—not an idea that we made up, but an idea that came before us and that we can fortunately discover, enter into, and explore without end. A practical faith will progressively lead us toward a surpassing reality, a secure reality not of our making.

Ultimately, we will gladly surrender all of our lesser ideas about what is real to this surpassing reality. The proof of progress along that spiritual route is a growing sense of inner security despite all the world's dangers and uncertainties.

FULFILLMENT. If stability and security were enough to satisfy the human spirit, we'd all be house pets. Clearly we are driven by a need to express ourselves, to be of use, and to achieve something, whether large or small, that symbolizes our unique characters.

In a world of so much struggle and confusion, the drive for fulfillment can easily get waylaid by silly, short-sighted, or destructive ambitions. Or it can become confused with the desire for security. The desire for personal wealth far beyond one's needs is just such a confusion between the legitimate desires for security and fulfillment.

I knew from childhood that I would be fulfilled through writing, but in my early adulthood I lost my instinctive sense of direction and no longer knew what to write about. So I focused for some years on the pursuit of economic security, with unimpressive results. Paradoxically, it was during a time of exceptional crisis—when I had lost virtually all my stability and security—that my drive for fulfillment unexpectedly reasserted itself, and I realized that I would begin writing again. My new subject matter was healing, particularly healing at the mind and spirit levels, the very kind of healing that was restoring my natural, long-lost faith to me.

Perhaps it is the bias of my experience that convinces me that all genuine fulfillment serves healing in some way. The very drive for fulfillment suggests that we are somehow unfulfilled, which means to me that we commonly experience a deficit of divine inspiration. To become whole is to recover that inspiration. If we look to conventional worldly goals like fame, riches, and influence, we are unlikely to find a lasting fulfillment, and may encounter great defeats and disillusionment along the way. Like faith, divine inspiration is something that comes from beyond us, but that we can invite into our experience, and thereafter follow its lead toward fulfillment.

At the lowest point of my health and spiritual crisis, I lay in a darkened room and said to myself earnestly, *"I give up my former life and accept the way of the heart."* I had borrowed the words from my spiritual readings, and I didn't know exactly what I was talking about. But I did have a compelling, twofold sense of surrender and invitation. I also had no idea of what would follow; I didn't even know if that moment would prove to be significant or if I would soon forget about it.

———————

Like faith, divine inspiration is something
that comes from beyond us, but that we can
invite into our experience, and thereafter
follow its lead toward fulfillment.

———————

In fact, what followed in the ensuing weeks and months were the first appreciable signs of improvement in my health, and unexpected inspirations and opportunities that would soon coalesce in my new writing career. (By the way, I've experienced many other moments of surrender and invitation since, and some have proven more significant than others. As with all forms of spiritual petitioning, practice increases productivity.)

Nowadays inspiration continues to arrive in the forms of unanticipated opportunities and unplanned undertakings, and I am amazed at my productivity in comparison to the years when I really wanted to be a writer but had no idea of whom or how my writing might serve. While there are still more things to try and some worldly goals I would like to achieve, I do not need to attain these objectives to find a far-off fulfillment; my fundamental fulfillment is always close at hand, in the work itself. Compared to the way I used to struggle for a sense of purpose and recognition, this feeling of inherent fulfillment in my work is quite literally a miracle of transformation.

For anyone who might worry that such fulfillment would result in complacency and creative stagnation, let me say that my experience is just the opposite. Authentic fulfillment is simultaneously complete in the moment, and always pulling one toward toward greater possibilities of service in the future. This feeling of "expanding complete-ness" is something I never experienced in my earlier, faith-deficient life, and I consider it a divine quality that surpasses the ego's sense of possibility. If anyone asked me how to start a new career, or become a writer or an artist or a rocket scientist, now I would say, "Find a way to surrender your ambitions and invite divine inspiration to help you learn to serve." Anyone who tried to follow this advice would necessarily have to develop some faith that there is such a mysterious and powerful thing as divine inspiration.

In this way faith makes fulfillment pos-sible—and a growing, authentic fulfillment certifies the practicality of faith.

When we feel stable, secure, and fulfilled, our deepest longings are answered and we arrive at a sense of completion, the feeling that we no longer need to search outside ourselves for something that has always been missing. When we know there is nothing missing within ourselves, we are truly at home in a world that may have felt like a strange and hostile territory before. It is a practical faith that delivers us to this sense of being at home—and it is a practical faith that can help us carry that home within us no matter what happens, and regardless of wherever we are led to serve during our stay on earth.

Without knowing it when I began, one of the reasons I have written this book is to celebrate the discovery of my own home within, the dynamic completion that I now feel where once there was a static and confused incompleteness. I hope that I have been practical enough in my words and faithful enough to my inspiration to help others find a faster route to their own homecoming. It is not merely possible to find a more faithful, loving, and sagacious way to live than we have known so far; it is our destiny, and it patiently awaits completion.

ABOUT THE AUTHOR

D. Patrick Miller is an author, writing coach, and literary agent and lives in Napa, California. His books include the *Understanding A Course in Miracles* and *The Forgiveness Book*.

Hampton Roads Publishing Company

. . . for the evolving human spirit

Hampton Roads Publishing Company publishes books on a variety of subjects, including spirituality, health, and other related topics.

For a copy of our latest trade catalog, call (978) 465-0504 or visit our distributor's website at *www.redwheelweiser.com*. You can also sign up for our newsletter and special offers by going to *www.redwheelweiser.com/newsletter/*.